Lali's Sleepover

by Arlène Elizabeth Casimir • illustrated by Mike Deas

Lucy Calkins and Michael Rae-Grant, Series Editors

LETTER-SOUND CORRESPONDENCES

m, t, a, n, s, ss, p, i,
d, g, o, c, k, ck, r, u,
h, b, e, f, ff, l, ll, z,
zz, j, v, w, y, x, -e,
-o, -y, ch

HIGH-FREQUENCY WORDS

is, see, the, too, of, says,
to, for, look, you, she, **do**

Lalin's Sleepover
Author: Arlène Elizabeth Casimir
Series Editors: Lucy Calkins and Michael Rae-Grant

Heinemann
145 Maplewood Avenue, Suite 300
Portsmouth, NH 03801
www.heinemann.com

Cataloging-in-Publication data is on file with the Library of Congress.

ISBN-13: 978-0-325-13836-7

Design and Production: Dinardo Design LLC, Carole Berg, and Rebecca Anderson

Editors: Anna Cockerille and Jennifer McKenna

Illustrations: Mike Deas

Photograph: p. 32 © Dejan Dundjerski/Shutterstock

Manufacturing: Gerard Clancy

Printed in Dongguan, China
4 5 6 7 8 9 10 TP 28 27 26 25 24 23
April 2023 Printing / PO# 4500868396

Contents

Meet...

Lalin

Tam

Ana

Sam

Nick

Imran

Lalin Sets Up

"A sleepover! A sleepover!"
says Lalin.

"Go set up the den
    for the sleepover," says Mom.
"I will jot a to-do list!"
    says Lalin.

"I can help you spell stuff,"
says Liv.

"Me too," says Bel.

"Do not help me!

I can do it!" huffs Lalin.

"Let Lalin do it," says Dad.

My list
- ☑ dust
- ☐ mats
- ☐ gift bags
- ☐ dolls
- ☐ blocks
- ☐ trucks
- ☐ kids

Lalin checks the top of the list.

It says "dust."

"OK, I will dust!" she says.

Lalin gets a rag

and gets rid of the dust.

Lalin checks the list.

It says "mats."

"OK, I will set up the mats!"
she says.

Lalin sets up

a bunch of mats.

She packs the gift bags.

She gets dolls, blocks, and trucks.

BUZZ!

BUZZ!

Lalin checks the list.

It says "kids."

"OK, I will let the kids in!"
she says.

2

Lalin's Sleepover

"The sleepover will be
so much fun!" says Lalin.

Lalin lets the kids in.

"Pick a spot for the sleepover,"
she says.

Lalin taps the bin.

"Let's play trucks," she says.

"It will be so much fun!"

"OK, but in a bit," says Ana.

The kids dress up the dolls
and stack up the blocks.

stomp!

Do the kids play trucks? No.

So Lalin gets a bit mad!

The kids look at Lalin.

"Is she mad?" asks Tam.

Sam hugs Lalin.

"Let's play trucks!" he says.

"OK," says Lalin.

"But let's play dolls
and blocks too.

It will be so much fun!"

3

At a Sleepover

Big kids can go to a sleepover.

It can be such fun!

Get your stuff
and pack up your bag!

Hug your pals
and set up your bed!

You can play with kids
at a sleepover.

You can see a film
at a sleepover.

You can snack,

and you can chat.

Zip into your bag
and get to bed!

A sleepover can be such fun!

COMPROMISE

First, we'll play dinos.

Then, we'll play blocks!

What do you do when you and your friend want to play different things? How do you agree? You *could* say, "No! I will only play my game!" But that's not a good way to be friends.

Instead, you could make a compromise. A *compromise* is like a deal, or an agreement. It's when you come up with an idea that works for everyone. One way to make a compromise is to *combine* your ideas and put them together, like Lalin and her friends. They combined trucks, dolls, and blocks so everyone could play. Another way to make a compromise is to *take turns*—do one idea first and then the next. Another way is to *go with the flow*. That means to do what your friend wants. Sometimes a friend really, really wants to play something. And sometimes you can let them, even if it's not your first choice.

Talk about...

Ask your reader some questions like...

- What happened in this book?
- What did Lalin do to get ready for the sleepover?
- Turn to page 19. Why was Lalin feeling a bit mad in this part?

- Turn to page 22. The kids make a *compromise*, a decision that works for everyone. Do you ever make a compromise when you're playing with friends? How?